9x 7/14 LT 6/14

There's an Opossum
in My Backyard

There's an Opossum in My Backyard

Gary Bogue
Illustrated by Chuck Todd

Heyday Books, Berkeley, California

Heyday Books, founded in 1974, works to deepen people's understanding and appreciation of the cultural, artistic, historic, and natural resources of California and the American West. It operates under a 501(c)(3) nonprofit educational organization (Heyday Institute) and, in addition to publishing books, sponsors a wide range of programs, outreach, and events.

To help support Heyday or to learn more about us, visit our website at www.heydaybooks.com, or write to us at P.O. Box 9145, Berkeley, CA 94709.

Library of Congress Cataloging-in-Publication Data

Bogue, Gary
  There's an opossum in my backyard / Gary Bogue ; Illustrated by Chuck Todd.
      p. cm.
  Includes bibliographical references.
  Summary: A baby opossum falls off its mother's back while traveling through the Green family's backyard and it spends the year there, learning about Rocky the dog, the cat next door, and the other wildlife in the yard. Includes facts about opossums, and related websites and books.
  ISBN 978-1-59714-059-1 (hardback : alk. paper)
  1. Opossums--Juvenile fiction. [1. Opossums--Fiction.] I. Todd, Chuck, ill. II. Title.
  PZ10.3.B6372Th 2007
  [E]--dc22
                              2006032667

Book design by Lorraine Rath

Printed in China by Oceanic Graphic Printing, Inc.

10 9 8 7 6 5 4 3 2 1

For Chantelle, Josh, Lauren, Mark, Megan,
and Monique, from Grandpa Gary
—*Gary Bogue*

To my little opossums Sienna and Sheridan,
the Vaughn family, and the Lindsay Wildlife Museum
—*Chuck Todd*

One morning a mother opossum was late getting back to her nest after a night of hunting for food. She was carrying her babies on her back. She ran along the top of a fence so hard that one of them bounced off. It landed on top of its tail and broke it. This left a kink in the very tip that would always make it easy to tell her apart from other opossums.

The mother opossum was in such a big hurry that she didn't even notice.

When the baby opossum fell into their backyard, the Greens were in the kitchen.

"Dad, Dad!" shouted Nathan. He ran to the window and pointed. "A baby rat just fell off that big rat's back!"

"That's an opossum, silly. It's a marsupial," said Ashley. She was Nathan's older sister, and she was very smart. "The females have pouches for their tiny babies, like kangaroos. The older babies ride on their mother's back, and if they fall off, she leaves them to grow up by themselves."

"It sure looks like a rat to me," said their father. "It also looks like it broke the end of its tail."

Nathan knew Ashley was right, but it was nice of Dad to agree with him.

The next morning, just as she did every day, Mrs. Green unlatched the dog door to let Rocky, the family dog, outside.

The little lost opossum was gobbling up dry dog food from a bowl on the patio when she heard the dog come rushing out. He started barking like crazy when he spotted her at his food dish. The little opossum opened her mouth wide, showing the dog her shiny, white, pointy teeth. Opossums don't like to fight, and showing off their teeth is usually all it takes to make another animal back off.

Meanwhile, the neighbor's big gray cat sat on the fence, watching quietly.

"Get away from my food!" Rocky barked at the opossum.

"Get away from *my* food!" the gray cat hissed at Rocky. It was a very big cat. It suddenly leaped at the dog. Rocky let out a big *yelp* and scurried back through his dog door.

The gray cat walked over and sniffed noses with the opossum over the dish of dog food.

"Do you mind if I join you?" purred the gray cat.

One night, while out for a stroll, the
opossum met some of her neighbors. It
was a warm night in the middle of July,
and lots of creatures were roaming around.
She sniffed noses with a skunk. "Boy,
do you smell," each of them thought.

A gopher snake hissed at her and told
her not to come too close.

A fat snail disappeared into its shell when
she sniffed at it with her pointy nose.

A huge raccoon ignored her.

A gopher took one look at her and dashed back down its hole.

The gray cat just sat on the fence, watching quietly.

ost nights, just before dark, the little opossum smelled something wonderful: the Greens cooking dinner.

One night she followed the delicious smell right up to Rocky's dog door. She had seen the dog use the swinging door many times. She pushed against it with her nose and followed the wonderful smell into the house.

"What are you doing in *my* house?"
barked Rocky.

He charged across the room at the
opossum. The opossum ran under a table.
The barking dog scrambled right after her.
They both ran under the chair where Ashley was reading.

Suddenly, there were feet everywhere. The opossum tried to run away from the dog. The dog tried to catch the opossum. Nathan tried to stop the dog. Ashley tried to block the doorway. Mr. and Mrs. Green jumped up from the kitchen table and joined the chase.

They all ended up in Nathan's room with the frightened little opossum hiding under his bed.

After things settled down, Mr. Green reached under the bed and scooped up the opossum into an empty shoebox.

"See the funny bend in its tail?" shouted Nathan. "It's our little opossum! What are you going to do with it?"

"I'm just going to take her home to the backyard," Dad said.

Several weeks later, the opossum was prowling around the backyard. As usual, she was looking for good things to eat. Once again, she smelled something very interesting. Her nose pointed up in the air as she followed the smell around to the side of the house, where she discovered that a raccoon had knocked the lid off the garbage can. She sniffed at the lid so loudly that the raccoon heard her. It poked its black-masked face up out of the can and looked down at her.

"What are you doing here?" it snarled. "This is *my* garbage can!"

In his bedroom, Nathan heard the snarl and sat straight up in bed. He tossed aside his covers, tiptoed over to the window, looked out, and saw the animals. He ran to his dresser, grabbed a flashlight, and slipped quietly out his bedroom door in his bare feet. He crept down the hall and out the back door.

The door made a loud, squeaky noise when he opened it.

The raccoon jumped out of the garbage can and ran away when it heard the door squeak. Nathan barely saw its ringed tail in the bright light of his flashlight.

Nathan heard another noise and
shined his flashlight on the garbage
can lid. "What are you doing here?"
Nathan smiled.

The opossum opened her mouth
and showed Nathan her fifty shiny,
white, pointy teeth.

"It's okay, little opossum," he said. "I won't hurt you." He stayed very quiet and turned the flashlight a little to the side so it wouldn't hurt her eyes.

The opossum closed her mouth and they just stared at each other. She remembered the times when she and the gray cat had sat and stared at each other, and suddenly she wasn't afraid.

Nathan shivered in the cold night air.
"Good night, little opossum, pleasant dreams,"
he said, and went back to his warm bed.

The opossum found her way into the garbage can and enjoyed the remains of the
Green family's dinner. Then she waddled off to sneak through Rocky's other dog door
into the Green family's garage. It was time to take a short nap in the warm nest she'd
made in some cardboard boxes by the end of the workbench.

Around five o'clock every morning, just before she climbed into her nest in the garage for the day, the opossum trotted across the street to hunt tasty earthworms on the neighbor's front lawn.

One morning, just as she reached the middle of the street, she heard a loud noise. Her eyes were blinded by two bright lights! She turned and opened her mouth to show the lights her shiny, white, pointy teeth.

"Whoa! Look out, little opossum!" shouted the driver of the car that was about to hit her. He was delivering newspapers. He swerved and barely missed her. "I wonder why they always open their mouths just before you hit them," he said to himself. He tossed a newspaper onto the Greens' driveway, shook his head, and drove down the street to the next driveway.

Where are all the different places in a yard that an opossum can look for food?

The dog's dish.
The garbage can.
Under the plum tree. It was nearing the end of
summer now, and there weren't many plums left.
Under the leaves, where crickets hide.
In the bushes, where treefrogs croak.
On the sidewalk, where the snails slide.
In the rocks, where alligator lizards live.
On the walls, where moths rest.

Early on another morning, just as the opossum was sniffing Rocky's food dish, she felt a strong gust of wind on her head. She turned to see where it was coming from. It was a great horned owl swooping down on her from a neighbor's palm tree!

She didn't have time to show it her teeth, so she jumped backwards. The clumsy young owl missed her and crashed into Rocky's food dish.

The young owl was furious. It clicked its top and bottom beaks together loudly, as owls often do when they are angry, and flew back up into the palm tree.

Rocky heard the clicking and the clatter and came barking
and yapping out through his dog door.

This was just too much for the opossum.
"Yipes!" she thought. And she fainted!

Sometimes when opossums are really frightened, they faint, and other times they just close their eyes and fall over and play dead. When an opossum does this, a little gland at the base of its tail squirts out a very stinky dead smell.

Rocky took a big sniff and walked away. Very fast.

The opossum got up and went looking for earthworms, and then she went to bed. She tucked herself into her cozy little nest of cardboard boxes and went to sleep.

It was the first day of school. Nathan and Ashley and Mr. and Mrs. Green were getting ready to drive to school.

While no one was looking, Nathan slipped over to where the opossum was sleeping. "Goodbye, little opossum," Nathan smiled. "I'll see you tonight."

The opossum opened one eye and looked up at Nathan. She didn't even open her mouth to show him her teeth. She just smiled a little opossum smile and closed her eye and went back to sleep.

One year later ...

A Few Words about Opossums

All these animals are marsupials. What do they have in common? A female marsupial carries and raises her babies in an external pouch on her abdomen.

koala bear

kangaroo

wallaby

Tasmanian devil

The Virginia opossum is the only native marsupial in North America.

Virginia opossum

When baby opossums are born, they are smaller than the tip of your little finger and not fully developed. They wiggle up the mother's furry stomach and into her pouch. Once inside they grab a nipple and start sucking.

The babies will live in the pouch for several months. When they get bigger and it gets too crowded, they will crawl out and ride around on the mother's back.

The opossum has a prehensile tail, which means it can curl around objects and hold onto them.

Opossums use their tails to grab branches and hang on tight so they won't fall out of trees.

They can drag and carry big bunches of dried grass and leaves with their tails to use for making nests. When they are still little, and not too heavy, baby opossums can hang from their mothers' tails.

Where to find out more about opossums

Websites:

The National Opossum Society; www.opossum.org

Windows on the Woodlands; www.flex.net/~lonestar/opossum.htm

Opossums; www.backyardnature.net/opossums.htm

Opossum Society; www.opossumsocietyus.org

Opossum Facts; http://opossum.craton.net

The Opossum: Our Marvelous Marsupial; www.wildliferescueleague.org/report/opossum.html

Books:

I Found a Baby Opossum; What Do I Do? by Dale Bick Carlson, Dale Carlson (Madison, Conn.: Bick Publishing House, 1997; ISBN 1884158064).

Opossum at Sycamore Road, by Sally M. Walker and illustrated by Joel Snyder (Washington, D.C.: Smithsonian Books, Smithsonian Backyard series, 1997; ISBN 1568994826).

Opossums, by Lynn M. Stone (Vero Beach, Fla.: Rourke Pub Group, The Nighttime Animals Series, 1993; ISBN 0865932956)

California Mammals, by E. W. Jameson Jr. and Hans J. Peeters (Berkeley: University of California Press, 1988, ISBN 0520052528).